Unit 1
Ireland

W0271068

1 A park in Dublin

a) Where in the picture is this? Write the correct letter.

1 on the right ____
2 at the bottom ____
3 behind the tree ____
4 on the left ____
5 in the background ____
6 in front of the tree ____
7 at the top ____
8 in the middle ____

b) Look at the picture in part a) and read the tip. Find other words for the words in red.

Tip If you don't know a word, don't worry. Use other words instead.

1 the weather is **hot** → ______________________ *(z. B. sehr warm)*
2 the woman is with **her son** → the woman is with a ______________ *(z. B. kleiner Junge)*
3 the boy **is crying** → the boy ______________________
4 the girls **are skipping** → ______________________

____

5 on the left is a man who is listening to **his MP3 player** → ______________________

____

6 at the bottom of the picture is **a car** which somebody has lost → ______________________

____

c) Now describe the picture in your exercise book. Write 100 words or more.

▸S. 8

2 a) The sad history of Dingle
Find the sentences.

Tip The text about Dingle on page 10 of your English book will help you to find the correct sentences.

1 Today Dingle	destroyed	because they had nothing to eat.
2 But in 1846 an awful thing	emigrated	a peaceful village in County Kerry.
3 A terrible disease	is	all the potatoes.
4 Some lucky people	happened	are still there.
5 But thousands of others	left behind	here and all over Ireland.
6 The ruined houses which they	starved	to the USA or Britain.

b) Write the sentences in your exercise book and make a text.
Put into your text three more things from the article on page 10 of your English book.

You can start like this: *The sad history of Dingle*
Today Dingle is a peaceful village in County Kerry. People still speak ...

▸ S. 10

3 Write the words in the puzzle.

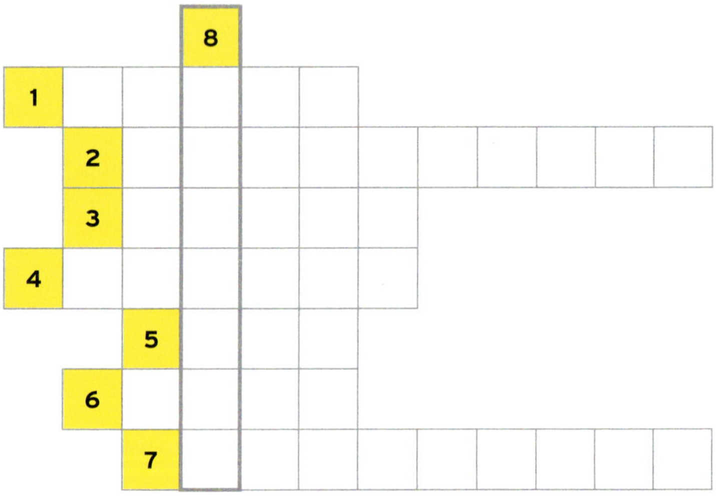

1 The Republic of Ireland and Northern Ireland are both in the European ...
2 In the 20th century Catholic and ... groups in Northern Ireland fought each other.
3 But now people don't fight – there's ... in Northern Ireland.
4 Like Olek, many people from ... and other countries work in Ireland.
5 More of the Irish population come from abroad than in ... other European country.
6 They don't ... come from Europe to work in Ireland – they come from China and the USA too.
7 But immigrants from the USA sometimes miss having ... for breakfast!

What's word 8? ______________________

▸ S. 11

• 4 A talk on Ireland
a) Write notes for each of these topics in your exercise book.

Example: *<u>Irish cities:</u> Dublin: capital, Republic of Ireland ...*

Irish cities | modern industry | historic events | people in Ireland

b) Use these notes to prepare a talk on one of the topics.
c) Now give your talk to a partner.

▸ S. 11

INTERPRETING

5 a) Jens's Irish friend, Liam, is from Belfast and has come to visit. Jens's cousin Lena wants to talk to Liam, but her English isn't very good. Jens interprets for them. What does he say?

LENA Ich war noch nie in Belfast. Wie ist es dort?

JENS ______

LIAM It's a really lively city and the nightlife is good.

JENS ______

LENA Es gibt also viele Angebote für junge Menschen?

JENS ______

LIAM Yes. There are two big concert halls. I saw four bands there last month.

JENS ______

LENA Die Titanic wurde doch in Belfast gebaut, oder? Ich habe den Film gesehen.

JENS ______

Tip
- You can understand new words or phrases if you know the parts, e.g.
  nightlife – you know night + life
  concert hall – you know concert + hall
- Remember:
  es gibt = there's/there are

LIAM Yes, Belfast was famous for shipbuilding. You must come and visit – it's a great city!

JENS ______

b) Practise interpreting the dialogue in groups of three people. The interpreter isn't allowed to look in a workbook.

▸ S. 13

READING – Adventures in Ireland

Tip You can use a dictionary.

1 My Irish girlfriend, Sue, and I live in New York. Last June she had an idea. "Tim, you're getting fat," she told me. "You need an adventure holiday. What about going to Ireland?" "Adventure? In Ireland? Are you crazy?" I replied. My picture of Ireland was green hills, quiet villages, no traffic and lots of sheep. All very nice ... for my grandparents. But not very exciting for young people, I thought. But do you know what? I was wrong!

2 We borrowed a friend's car in Dublin and toured the country, starting in the south. Our first stop was Blarney Castle just outside Cork, the republic's second largest city. Here, I knew, tourists kiss the Blarney Stone: the legend says that if you kiss the stone, you'll talk well and easily all your life. What I didn't know was that in order to kiss the stone you have to lie on your back and lean backwards over the edge of a very high tower. It was scary!

3 "What about sea kayaking?" said Sue the next day. Well, I couldn't say no, could I? Sea kayaking is really exciting, I can tell you! The waves push you right and left, and up and down. When I went up I could see cliffs and little islands with seals on them; when I went down I couldn't see the coast or any other boat, only an enormous wave in front of me and that was frightening. But sea kayaking is an amazing experience!

4 What was next? Well, two days later we joined ten other people on a speedboat to the Skellig Islands – two pyramids of rock, ten miles out in the ocean. Nobody, I thought, could live on these islands – but I was wrong. Monks had built a tiny monastery here in the sixth century and had lived here for six hundred years. "How on earth did the monks get to the islands?" I wondered. "They rowed," answered the guide. "And they prayed." Well, I could understand that! First I thought that there was snow on the islands – but it wasn't snow: it was thousands and thousands of white birds! On one of the islands you climb six hundred steps and then you suddenly see a row of ancient huts. They're made of stone and look very strange, like something out of Lord of the Rings. When you climb to the top of the tiny island, you feel that you're standing alone in the middle of the ocean. You can't hear anything except the wind, the waves and the sea birds.

5 Further north along the coast we came to a flat but rocky region called the Burren. Everything was grey here: the rocks, the sky and the fog. In the fog we visited some very old tombs. They looked really spooky. Fortunately the sun shone again when we went down to the beach. We couldn't swim (it was too cold!) but we hired horses and rode for three hours on the wide, empty beach – we felt like cowboys! (But my whole body hurt after the ride!)

6 Our next stop was Achill Island, or *Oileán Acaill* in Gaelic, where many people still speak Gaelic. It's a beautiful island with an adventure centre where you can learn surfing, mountain climbing and abseiling. We tried abseiling – it was great fun! Then we travelled north again and stopped at the Slieve League Cliffs in the north west of Ireland. They are some of the highest cliffs in Europe and a crazy road with scary hairpin bends[1] leads you to a car park. From there Sue had to help me on the hair-raising[2] path along the edge of the cliffs, because I didn't dare to look down. I felt so stupid!

7 We then crossed the border into Northern Ireland and saw the Giant's Causeway, which was phenomenal. It's like a road which leads into the sea, made of perfect hexagonal stones. It's amazing that nature can produce stones which are so regular! And not far away is the crazy Carrick-a-rede rope bridge: a bridge 25 metres above the sea. It leads to a tiny island and, as it's made of rope, it swings in the wind, and it goes up and down when people walk across it. This time it was Sue who was scared so I held her arm and helped her across.

8 Our final stop before Dublin was Belfast, the city where the *Titanic* was built in 1912, and where we saw some of the strangest tourist sights of our whole trip. For thirty years to 1998, terrorists fought each other in the streets of Belfast. Protestants and Catholics painted the sides of houses with enormous propaganda paintings. The fighting has now stopped and the colourful murals ... have become tourist sites!

6 Find a title for each paragraph 1–8. You won't need two titles.

Paragraph	1	2	3	4	5	6	7	8
Title								

A Two rocky islands
B What visitors do in a castle
C Ireland's most modern building
D A historical visit and fun by the seaside
E Tourist sights produced by years of fighting
F A village where life has not changed
G Two sights in Northern Ireland
H False ideas about Ireland
I Alone in a small boat in the sea
J A spectacular road and a dangerous path

▸ S. 16

[1] hairpin bend [heəpɪn bend] *Haarnadelkurve* [2] hair-raising [heəreɪzɪŋ] *haarsträubend, furchterregend*

7 **True, false or not in the text? Tick (✔) the right answer.**

	True	False	Not in text
1 Tim was surprised when his girlfriend suggested a holiday in Ireland.	☐	☐	☐
2 Blarney Castle is near Cork.	☐	☐	☐
3 There was snow on the Skellig Islands when Tim visited them.	☐	☐	☐
4 Tim and his girlfriend went swimming before they hired horses on the beach.	☐	☐	☐
5 Lots of tourists were looking at Belfast's propaganda paintings when Tim was there.	☐	☐	☐

8 **Explain the following words in English. You can use a dictionary.**

1 a speedboat (*line 27*) – *a fast boat with a motor*
2 a monastery (*line 30*) – *a place where* ____________________
3 a tomb (*line 47*) – ____________________
4 swings (*line 65*) – ____________________
5 a mural (*line 74*) – ____________________

9 **Answer these questions in full sentences.**

1 Why did Tim think Ireland was a bit boring? His picture ____________________
____________________.
2 What did Sue and Tim do and see on the Skellig Islands? They ____________________
____________________.
3 What did they visit in the Burren? ____________________
4 How did they feel at Carrick-a-rede? ____________________

• **10** **Tim and Sue were sometimes a bit frightened during their holiday in Ireland.**
Example: *Tim was a bit frightened when he kissed the Blarney Stone because he had to lean backwards over the edge of a high tower.*

a) Give three other examples – and explain why Tim or Sue was frightened.

b) And you? When have you been frightened? What happened? Write 60 words or more in your exercise book.

► S. 16

LISTENING

11 St Patrick is Ireland's patron saint[1] and St Patrick's Day is Ireland's most famous festival. Listen to the radio interview and take notes.

1 What date is St Patrick's Day? ______

2 Why is this day St Patrick's Day? ______

______

3 What colour do many people wear at St Patrick's Day parades? Why?

______

4 How long does the St Patrick's Day festival in Dublin last? ______

5 Where does the biggest St Patrick's Day parade in the world take place? ______

6 When's the St Patrick's Day festival in Munich? ______

______

► S. 17

12 a) Listen to the radio programme about a holiday with horse and caravan.

1 What kind of radio programme is this?

☐ a) an interview ☐ b) a comedy ☐ c) an advert ☐ d) a news report

2 What's in the caravan?

☐ a) a television ☐ b) a motor ☐ c) sport equipment ☐ d) some furniture

• b) Listen again and note five details.

______
______
______
______
______
______
______
______

• 13 Would you like to go on a holiday with horse and caravan in Ireland? Why? Why not?
a) Write 100 words in your exercise book.
b) Then talk to a partner about that kind of holiday.

► S. 17

[1] patron saint ['peɪtrən seɪnt] *Schutzpatron*

MEDIATION

11 October
Raising money for good causes

Last Saturday I played in a concert at our school. It was really brilliant and we had lots of fun too! We wanted to raise money for good causes. We're going to send the money to Africa, to help fight poverty and HIV/Aids. Every year more people need money for food and drugs.

I think people in this country are often too selfish and only spend their money on themselves. Some people think I'm too idealistic. Well, I'm not completely naive – I know that a bunch of kids in Ireland can't solve the world's problems. But I think it's important to try. And lots of top celebrities think so too.

Next week we're baking cakes. We're going to sell them at break and I hope we'll make lots of money!

14 a) Read the blog. It's written by an Irish teenager. Then find words 1–6 and tick the right meaning for each sentence.

Tip Lots of words have more than one meaning. When you use a dictionary, choose the right meaning for the sentence!

1	brilliant	☐ *Adjektiv* glänzend	☐ *Adjektiv* strahlend	☐ *Adjektiv* großartig
2	drug	☐ *Verb* betäuben	☐ *Nomen* Medikament	☐ *Nomen* Droge
3	bunch	☐ *Nomen* Strauß	☐ *Nomen* Bund	☐ *Nomen* Haufen, Gruppe
4	top	☐ *Adjektiv* größte	☐ *Nomen* Verschluss	☐ *Nomen* Gipfel
5	break	☐ *Verb* brechen	☐ *Verb* unterbrechen	☐ *Nomen* Pause
6	make	☐ *Nomen* Marke	☐ *Verb* bewirken	☐ *Verb* verdienen

b) Write these phrases from the text in German. Check the word order.

Tip Remember, English word order is different from German! E.g.
yesterday I went to a concert
gestern bin ich zu einem Konzert gegangen

1 last Saturday I played in a concert

2 every year more people need money

3 next week we're baking cakes

c) Now translate the text into German.

▸S. 18

WRITING – A picture story

15 **This story is often told in Ireland. People say that it happened in 1949. Use the pictures and tell the story. Write at least 120 words in your exercise book.**

> **Tip** Use the right forms of the verbs. E.g.
> – *past progressive*: Mick Ryan was driving
> – *simple past*: when he saw

The story of Mick Ryan

▸ S. 19

16 **Finish the story. Write at least 120 words.**

> **Tip** You could describe
> - what the weather was like, e.g. It was cold and ...
> - what happened, e.g. Suddenly the horse ...
> - what they did and thought, e.g. Niklas followed ...
> - what happened next, e.g. Later they found ...
> - what they did in the evening, e.g. They tried to ...

A holiday in Ireland

Last summer Niklas and Katharina went on holiday to Ireland. They didn't want a boring holiday on the beach, so they chose something very different: a holiday with a horse and caravan.

The first day was great. The sun shone, the horse was friendly and the caravan was comfortable.

But on the second day everything changed ...

▸ S. 19

17 **Finish Katie's email with verbs in the *past perfect*.**

The swimming competition in Cork was a disaster! We arrived late. Dad *hadn't driven* (*not drive*) to Cork before and the road was busier than he ______________ (*think*). When we arrived I felt so stupid – I ______________ (*leave*) my swimming costume at home! I ______________ (*tell*) Dad to put my bag in the car, but he ______________ (*not hear*) me. So we ______________ (*go*) all the way for nothing!

▶ S. 21

18 **a) Ryan and his mum**
Circle the right form of the verbs. Do you need the *simple past* or the *past perfect*?

When Ryan came home yesterday, he was / had been tired because he played / had played football all afternoon. His mum was / had been angry, because Ryan fell / had fallen and his clothes were really dirty. "And did you remember to go shopping for me?" she asked / had asked. But Ryan forgot / had forgotten. "That's it! You're staying at home for a week!" said / had said his mum.

Do you think Ryan's mum was fair? Yes / No

▶ S. 21

● **b) What happens if you're late? What do your parents do or say? Tell a partner.**

19 **A bad day for Patrick**
Write sentences with the *past perfect* and the *simple past*.

	❶	→	❷	
1	phone new girlfriend	→	have lunch	*After I had phoned my new girlfriend, I had lunch.*
2	drink coffee	→	work in garden	*After I* ______________ .
3	plant potatoes	→	pick flowers for girlfriend	*After* ______________ .
4	wash	→	take flowers to girlfriend	______________ .
5	see her with another boy	→	throw flowers away	______________ .

▶ S. 21

20 Irish castles
Tick the right words.

Ireland has ☐ lots / ☐ many / ☐ much castles and they are ☐ enormous / ☐ enormously important for the Irish tourist industry. Tourists always find them ☐ interest / ☐ interested / ☐ interesting and they love ☐ visit / ☐ visiting / ☐ visited them. Leap Castle is ☐ famous / ☐ famously for its ghosts, while tourists ☐ who / ☐ which visit Blarney Castle want ☐ kiss / ☐ to kiss / ☐ kissing the Blarney Stone. Some castles, like Tullynally Castle, are homes for families that ☐ live / ☐ lived / ☐ have lived there for centuries. ▸S. 23

21 Find the right noun for each verb.

1 Some people *babysit* for neighbours at the weekend.
But I'm not old enough to be a ________________.

2 My parents love *walking* in the country.
On Sundays we all go for a long ____________.

3 I *read* two or three books a week.
______________ is my favourite hobby.

4 Last summer I read ten books on holiday. We *camped* in Ireland.
The __________________________ was near a wood.

5 My dad *built* us a tree-house in the wood.
There was also an old _______ in the middle of the wood.

▸S. 23

22 a) Odd one out
Which word is different? Cross it out.

1 tent – hotel – ~~holiday~~ – caravan
2 coach – driver – ambulance – lorry
3 teacher – viewer – pilot – scientist
4 honest – confident – happy – pessimistic
5 break – crash – repair – explode

b) Write two more odd one out puzzles for a partner.

____

____

▸S. 23

1 My family

Which words do you need?
Put in the right words – in English.

auswandern • besitzen • Grundbesitzer
pachten • pflanzen • Vorfahren

Tip In some sentences you'll need the *simple past*.

1 I'm American but my ______________ are Irish.
2 They ______________ to the USA in 1854.
3 In Ireland they had to ______________ their land
4 from a ______________, but in the USA
5 they were able to ______________ some land.
6 They ______________ vegetables and they soon had a successful business.

6 points

2 Which syllables do you stress? Say these words, then put them in the right box.

celebrity • enormously • European • idealistic • industry • injustice
minority • Netherlands • population • president • Protestant • republic

O o o	o O o	o O o o	o o O o
company	important	receptionist	independent
______	______	______	______
______	______	______	______
______	______	______	______
______	______	______	______

6 points

3 My grandparents

Write the right form of the verbs: *simple past / past perfect / past continuous*.

1 come — My grandparents ______________ to California from New York in 1963.
2 meet • marry — They ______________ six years before and ______________ in 1959,
3 live — while they ______________ in New York.
4 have — They ______________ their first child, my father, in California.
5 work — My grandfather ______________ as taxi-driver when my father was born.

6 points

Auf Seite 61 findest du die Lösungen.

Unit 2

South Africa

1 You can see these wild animals at the Kruger National Park. Write their names. Use a dictionary for the animals you don't know.

▸S. 24

2 These sentences are false. Write correct sentences.

> **Tip** Think about *which* words you need to change, e.g. doesn't have → has or → and

1 South Africa doesn't have good railways or roads.

South Africa has ______________________________.

2 All the houses in the poorest suburbs have running water.

____

____

3 Nobody in the poor parts of the country suffers from AIDS.

____

4 Cricket is South Africa's most popular sport.

____

5 The country has only one language and culture.

____

▸S. 25

3 Do you think it was a good idea to have the 2010 football World Cup in South Africa? Why?/Why not?

____

____

▸S. 25

4 a) Apartheid in South Africa
Which parts go together? Fill in the numbers. One example (0) is already given.

0	Before 1994		to different schools		marry		at a peaceful protest.
1	Black children went		of the 1980s		the first black	0	to vote.
2	Black people	0	black people		unarmed Blacks		president in 1994.
3	In 1960		became		there was more		badly-paid jobs.
4	By the end		couldn't	0	weren't allowed		and more violence.
5	Nelson Mandela		white police fired at		and then got		white people.

b) Write the sentences and make a text. Put into your text three more things from page 26 of your English book.

▸S. 26

You can start like this: *Apartheid in South Africa*
Before 1994 black people weren't allowed to vote. They had to live in special areas called ...

Tip
- The words are on pages 24–27 of your English book.
- Each answer has an 'o' in it.

5 What are the right words?

1 It's a sort of music. ______
2 It's a big football competition. ______
3 It's a sort of bird, but it can't fly. ______
4 It's what school gives you. ______
5 You sometimes see it in the sky. It has lots of colours. ______
6 They're small but very expensive and some people wear them in a ring or earrings. ______

▸S. 27

• 6 a) The old system of apartheid in South Africa was very unfair. Do black and white people have the same lifestyles now?
Give reasons for your answer. Write 50–80 words.

b) Compare your answer with your partner's.

▸S. 27

READING – South African TV

TUESDAY, 8 APRIL 2009

SABC 1

18.30 360 Degrees (Live)
360 Degrees is an information-packed news and current affairs show with a strong bias towards opinion and decision makers.

19.00 Zola 7
Hosted by actor, recording artist and youth celebrity, Zola, each show revolves around the story of one person who is preparing for a day that will have a huge impact on their lives. It's a dream come true, a day in their lives they will never forget.

19.30 Muvhango
Episode 35: Lebo and Dineo have an argument about their roles at work. Mulimisi surprises Lufuno with a visit. She's never met him before and she's entranced by this handsome man. James is annoyed when he finds Meme being friendly with Alilali and he tells Alilali what he thinks of her.

20.00 Hotspot
Videos from local and international bands and solo artists.

SABC 2

18.30 7de Laan
Episode 82: Dawid sees Amanda in the Deli. Lukas asks Clara to have dinner with him.

19.00 More 4 U
This week: braai recipes. Learn how to make perfect braai bread, BBQ sauce and the traditional boerewors.

19.30 Know Your Game
Most people taking part in sports suffer injuries at some point. This programme gives viewers an opportunity to learn more about different sports injuries: how they happen and how to prevent and treat them.

20.00 The Golden Way
Young police officer Sean "Coop" Cooper works the streets dealing with drug offenders. When Coop's body is found in a bad neighbourhood, theories range from revenge to a gang killing to a jealous lover. But D I Golden's investigation uncovers a secret about Coop that may have motivated someone entirely unexpected to murder him.

7 a) Look at this South African TV programme. Find programmes that these five people might like to watch. Write the name(s) of the programme(s).

Tip Look through the information quickly. You don't need to understand every word to do the task.

1 Klaas likes cooking. ______
2 Naledi is interested in politics. ______
3 Antjie likes soap operas. ______
4 Uuka goes jogging every day. ______
5 Corika likes reality TV. ______

b) What are the names of the other two programmes? Write what they are about.

1 ______
2 ______

▸S. 32

READING – Steve Biko, an anti-apartheid activist

A But the peaceful demonstration in Soweto became violent: many Blacks were killed when the police fired at the unarmed crowd. These protests began the Black revolution which only ended years later when the black leader Nelson Mandela came out of prison.

B The world was shocked by the death of Steve Biko who had always protested peacefully. Because of his death even more people worked against apartheid.

C Steve Biko was born on 18th December 1946 and he became one of the black leaders who fought against apartheid in the 1960s and 1970s. His slogan “black is beautiful” became world-famous.

D The BCM became very popular and in 1976 it helped to organise protests against the government. The protests took place in the black suburb of Soweto, a part of Johannesburg, when the government told black people that maths lessons in schools now had to use Afrikaans, not English. On 16th June thousands of students began a peaceful demonstration.

E A year after the 1976 protests in Soweto, the government arrested Steve Biko. The police treated him with violence. He was beaten and chained to a window for a day. Then he was transported, without clothes, 1500 kilometres in the back of a Land Rover to a prison hospital in Pretoria. He was already nearly dead. Biko died soon after he arrived in hospital – but the government said that he had tried to kill himself.

F As a young man, Biko became involved in politics at the university of Natal, where he was a student. The main black organisation in South Africa was the ANC, but after the Sharpeville Massacre in 1960 many of its leaders were in prison. The Blacks needed new leaders and Biko organised a new anti-apartheid organisation called the Black Consciousness Movement (BCM).

8 **a) Read these paragraphs about Steve Biko and put them in the correct order.**

1	2	3	4	5	6
C					

b) Find the right word for the definition.

1 a ________________ is when people protest about something

2 a ________________ is a large group of people

3 a ________________ is a place where criminals are sent

4 a ________________ is where ill people are looked after

▸S. 32

9 Mark the correct ending with a cross[1] (X).

1 Black protests in South Africa only ended when ...	☐	the police fired at the crowd in Soweto.
	☐	Nelson Mandela went to prison.
	☐	Nelson Mandela was freed from prison.
2 Steve Biko's birthday was on the ...	☐	25th July.
	☐	18th December.
	☐	16th June.
3 In 1976 there was a protest in ...	☐	a suburb of Johannesburg.
	☐	Sharpeville.
	☐	Natal.
4 Steve Biko died in ...	☐	1960.
	☐	1976.
	☐	1977.
5 The BCM was ...	☐	a government organisation.
	☐	an organisation that fought apartheid.
	☐	the prison Steve Biko was sent to.

10 Find the opposites in the article:

1 peaceful – ____________________

2 began – ____________________

3 never – ____________________

4 died – ____________________

5 before – ____________________

6 with – ____________________

• 11 Steve Biko said:

"It is better to die for an idea that will live than to live for an idea that will die".

a) What does this sentence mean in German?

b) Do you agree? Why? Why not?

Your answer should have at least 50 words.

c) Discuss your opinion with a partner.

▸ S. 32

[1] mark with a cross [mɑːk wɪð ə krɒs] *ankreuzen*

LISTENING

12 **a) Listen to some information about the people of South Africa. Tick the topics that you hear information about.**

☐ *hobbies* ☐ *population* ☐ *food*

☐ *education* ☐ *disease* ☐ *languages*

b) Listen again and complete the table.

	South Africa 	Germany 
population	48 million	____ million
children (0–14 years)	____ %	____ %
people over 65 years	____ %	____ %
adults who can read and write	____ %	____ %
people who have finished high school	Whites: ____ % Blacks: ____ %	

► S. 33

13 **What's the capital of South Africa? There are three capitals! Listen and write the name of the town. Then write the number of the town (1–3) next to the right information.**

Tip There are sometimes two answers.

Name of town		Where it is		Why it's a capital
① _ _ _ _ _ _ _ _	☐	in the centre	☐	the president lives there
② _ _ _ _ _ _ _ _	☐	in the south	☐	it's the biggest city
③ _ _ _ _ _ _ _ _ _ _ _ _ _	☐	in the north	☐	it has the parliament
	☐	in the east	☐	the president works there
	☐	on the coast	☐	the most important court is there

► S. 33

MEDIATION – Your uncle wants to visit Kruger National Park.

14 **You find some information about the different seasons there on the Internet. Read the information and translate it into German. Write the translation in your exercise book. The tips will help you and you can use a dictionary too.**

KRUGER NATIONAL PARK THROUGH THE YEAR

The best time for seeing wildlife in Kruger National Park is the winter season, when there isn't much rain. At this time visitors are easily able to see the animals, which have to come to the waterholes because they need water to drink. They come in the mornings and evenings. The grass is short and the trees don't have leaves, so visitors have a good view of the area and the animals.

September to October is spring, and the height of the dry season with hot dry winds. The rivers are low.

Visitors, who come in November and December, often find it too hot and there are sometimes storms in the afternoon. This is the rainy season in Kruger Park. The rains quickly fill the rivers and waterholes and the bush looks very green. Seeing animals is difficult in the summer season because the trees have a lot of leaves. However, many animals are born during this time.

In April the thick green bush becomes thinner and brown. This is Kruger's autumn period. The temperatures start getting colder at night but during the day it is still warm. For visitors this is probably the most difficult time of the year if they want to see animals in Kruger National Park because the grass is dense and high. On the other hand many birds can be seen.

Tip Remember:
write a rough translation (*Rohübersetzung*) first.
Then check it:
- Does it sound right?
- Can you make it better?

when; at this time … – Achte auf die deutsche Wortstellung
waterhole – Wasserloch

because … – Wortstellung
are born – Passiv: werden … geboren

in April … – Wortstellung

can be seen – Passiv: können … gesehen werden

► S. 34

WRITING

15 **Read the notes (A–D) and write sentences about Lesedi and his girlfriend.**
Tips 1–10 will help you write better sentences.

> **Tip** Remember to write your story in the *simple past*.

A Lesedi • phone • new girlfriend Puleng
uncle • give • tickets • cricket match

Last Friday evening Lesedi phoned his new

> **Tips**
> 1 start with a time phrase, e.g. last Friday evening
> 2 join *(verbinde)* the sentences with because
> 3 use the *past perfect* (had given him)

B Puleng think • cricket • boring
say yes • spend day with Lesedi

> **Tips**
> 4 What did the people say? use *if* ..., e.g. "If you come, you'll enjoy it."
> 5 join the sentences: Although Puleng thought ..., she said
> 6 use adverbs, e.g. incredibly / really boring

C go to • match • start 10 a.m.

> **Tip**
> 7 join parts with which

D arrive • nobody there
tickets for *next* week

> **Tips**
> 8 start with but when
> 9 use an adverb, e.g. unfortunately
> 10 say how they felt

▸ S. 35

16 **Open-ended story**
Read the start of the story. Then look at the blue box. You can use the ideas to finish the story. Write at least 120 words.

> **Tip** Use ideas from the tips above.

Late for the cinema
Lesedi and his girlfriend Puleng wanted to see the latest film. It started at 6.45 p.m. They decided to meet at Puleng's house at 5 p.m. on Sunday and take the bus into town ...

- Lesedi late: why?
- wait – bus stop
- bus slow: why?
- walk – rain: soon both wet
- arrive at cinema 7.30 p.m.
- new plan for the evening: what?

▸ S. 35

17 What does the South African guide tell the tourists about their day trip? Fill in the right verbs. (You won't need all of the verbs.)

→ drive • go • has • leaves • offer • return • stops • try • visit

Our coach ________ at 8.30 a.m. and we ________ 95 km to the town of Oudtshoorn. In the morning we ________ a monkey and hippo park, where you'll be able to have your photo taken with one of the monkeys. At midday the coach ________ at an ostrich ranch, where you can eat ostrich steaks. In the afternoon we ________ on a guided tour of the ranch. We ________ to the hotel at around 5.30 p.m.

▸ S. 36

18 a) Plans for the weekend
Write the conversation in sentences.
Use the *present progressive*.

Tip Remember: at the weekend
on Friday (morning)
in the evening

EMMA *what – do – weekend?*
What are you doing ________________________?

JOHN *Saturday – work – restaurant*
____

evening – watch – sister
____

she – play – in – badminton match
____

EMMA *what – do – Sunday?*
____

JOHN *Sunday morning – homework*
____

afternoon – grandma – come for tea
____

b) Now write about Emma's plans for the weekend. Make up the details.
You can start like this: *On Saturday morning she's ...*

▸ S. 37

19 Sounds
Put the words in the correct boxes.

→ aid • coast • doughnut • eight • friend • hometown • lots • mall • only
peace • railway • teenager • thief • wash • wave • wealthy • when

[əʊ]	[eɪ]	[iː]	[ɒ]	[e]
most	late	free	was	ten
______	______	______	______	______
______	______	______	______	______
______	______	______	______	______
______	______	______	______	______
______	______	______	______	______

▸ S. 39

20 What do the words in red mean? Explain them in English.

1 A shop assistant is someone ______.
2 When someone is unemployed, he or she ______.
3 A postman is someone ______.
4 Your cousin is ______.
5 A pet is ______.

▸ S. 39

• **21 Mixed tenses**
Complete the sentences. Use the right forms of the verbs.

1 LEFU What (*you – do*) ______ last weekend?
2 JOE (*we – go*) ______ on a tour of Robben Island.
3 LEFU (*I – never – be*) ______ to Robben Island.
4 JOE (*it – be*) ______ really interesting.
5 (*my mum – tell*) ______ me about Nelson Mandela before the visit.
6 LEFU (*we – go*) ______ there next weekend, when my cousins come to stay.
7 JOE I'm sure (*you – enjoy*) ______ yourselves.
8 LEFU Yes, (*my cousins – be*) ______ very interested in politics and history.

▸ S. 39

1 Read the phonetic script and write the names of these animals in English

1 ['mʌŋki] ____________ 2 ['bʌfələʊ] ____________ 3 ['elɪfənt] ____________

4 ['lepəd] ____________ 5 ['laɪən] ____________ 6 ['raɪ'nɒsərəs] ____________

3 points

2 South Africa today
Read the text and write the missing words.

South Africa is often called the rainbow ____________ because of all the different cultures of the people ____________ live there. The ____________ speak English or Afrikaans which is a language like ____________. The Blacks speak more than nine ______________ languages.
But South Africa still ______ problems. Unemployment has been __________ down but 23 % of people still have no _____. Only 74.4 % of houses have ______________ water and 20 % of houses don't have ______________ light.

10 points

3 Jacob asks Amy what she's doing at the weekend. Look at the pictures and write Amy's answers in sentences in the *present progressive*.

____
____
____
____
____
____

____
____
____
____
____
____

8 points

Makhaya Ntini – a short biography

Makhaya Ntini is South African teenagers' most popular sports star, according to a survey of young people. Born on 6th July 1977 Ntini made history when he became the first black player to play for the South African national cricket team.

Ntini came from a poor family. He was looking after cattle in his home village of Mdingi in the south-east of the country when people first realised that he had a great talent for sport, especially cricket. The boy was sent away to Dale College in King William's Town to learn to be an even better player.

Cricket is South African young people's second favourite sport after football. Rugby and athletics come third and fourth. The South African cricket team is one of the best in the world. They often play against Australia, India and England.

In 2008 Ntini founded a cricket school to help poor and disadvantaged young boys who want to play cricket for South Africa.

As well as playing for the South African team, Ntini plays cricket for the Chennai Super Kings in the Indian Premier League.

4 a) Read the article. Are the statements true, false or not in the text? Tick the right answer.

	Statement	True	False	Not in text
1	Makhaya Ntini is a cricket player.	☐	☐	☐
2	There were many black players in the South African team before Ntini.	☐	☐	☐
3	Ntini's family had a lot of money.	☐	☐	☐
4	Ntini completed all his education in his home village.	☐	☐	☐
5	He's married and has children.	☐	☐	☐
6	Cricket is the most popular sport with South African teenagers.	☐	☐	☐
7	Ntini's new cricket school is in his hometown.	☐	☐	☐
8	At the moment Ntini plays for an Indian team.	☐	☐	☐

8 points

b) Numbers
Find the words in the text.

1st ________ 2nd ________ 3rd ________

4th ________ ________ sixth

2,5 points

Auf den Seiten 61–62 findest du die Lösungen.

India

1 Listen again to the text from your English book. Complete these sentences.

Tip Read the sentences before you listen, so you know what information you're looking for. Listen carefully! The speaker won't say the same words that are in this exercise.

1 A *sitar* is an Indian musical instrument. It's like a ______________.

2 The sitar has been played for ______________________________ in India.

3 Indian culture is very old. The first ______________ were built 4500 years ago.

4 80 % of Indians are ________________ – probably the oldest religion in the world.

5 India has over _____________ different languages.

6 India has more English-speaking people than ____________!

7 Over 30 % of India's population is ______________ ______________.

8 India's ______________________ is the largest in the world.

▸ S. 40

2 What do you know about India? Circle the right answers.

1 India's border with Pakistan is in the *north-west / north-east / south-east*.

2 The Taj Mahal is India's most famous *department store / Bollywood film / building*.

3 Project Tiger was founded in 1972 because tigers were *dangerous / everywhere / almost extinct*.

4 At the moment the number of tigers in India is *staying the same / going up / going down*.

5 India has the second biggest population *in the world / in Asia / in Europe*.

6 Mumbai is a very large city with a population of 19 *billion / million / thousand*.

7 Streets in Indian cities are *wide / quiet / busy*.

8 70 % of Indians live in *cities / villages / Mumbai*.

9 Most villages now have *a nature reserve / a fast food restaurant / running water*.

10 Monsoon rains often *cause floods / help crops / bring good luck*.

▸ S. 41

3 Look at pages 40–43 in your English book. Explain in English:

What is ...

1 Bollywood? It's ______________________.

2 an arranged marriage? It's when ______________________

______________________.

3 the monsoon season? It's when ______________________.

4 child labour? It's when ______________________

______________________.

5 a mother language? It's ______________________.

6 cholera? It's ______________________.

▸ S. 43

4 Complete these sentences using the passive. Which tense do you need: the *simple present* or the *simple past*?

1 (*download*) Katrina Kaif's films *are* ______________ more than any other actor's in India.

2 (*build*) The Taj Mahal *was* ______________ in the 17th century by an Muslim prince.

3 (*arrange*) Most Indian marriages ______________ by the young people's parents.

4 (*start*) Project Tiger ______________ by people who wanted to protect tigers.

5 (*call*) Mumbai ______________ Bombay when it was a British colony.

6 (*damage*) Often, crops in India ______________ by floods during the monsoon season.

7 (*speak*) In India English ______________ as a second language by many people.

8 (*destroy*) In 2008 many homes ______________ by terrible floods in Bihar.

▸ S. 43

5 Write a short text about Bipasha Basu, one of Bollywood's most famous stars.

Name:	Bipasha Basu
Height:	172 cm
Born:	7 January 1979, Delhi
Religion:	Hindu
Family:	two sisters
Work:	model, Bollywood actress
Education:	secondary school; college
Hobbies:	singing and dancing
First film:	Ajnabee
Favourite colour:	pink
Favourite place:	Paris

▸ S. 43

READING – A travel blog

BUSY DAYS IN INDIA

Asia → India → Delhi

by *Martin Blackmore*
3 February

Well, here I am in Delhi, at last! I thought London was busy – but Delhi must be the busiest city in the world. It's certainly very noisy. The narrow streets are packed with people, cars, bikes – and even cows and elephants! It's really hard just to cross the road. All around you are people who want to sell you things and they keep trying, even if you say 'no' a hundred times. It's an amazing city, but pretty tiring. And I hate to see so many very poor people begging for money in the streets. Fortunately, English is widely-spoken here.

It's still the winter season here and the temperature is just right for seeing the sights – it's 22 °C at the moment. In May and June, the hottest months of the summer, it goes up to 40 degrees or more in Delhi. I wouldn't like to come here then ...

AWESOME TAJ MAHAL

Asia → India → Agra

7 February

I've come to Agra, a city 200 km south of Delhi, to see the world-famous Taj Mahal. And I haven't been disappointed: it's truly awesome. No wonder three million people visit it every year! It was built in the seventeenth century by a Muslim prince for his third and favourite wife, Mumtaz Mahal. She died when their fourteenth (yes, *fourteenth*!) child was born. The prince built the Taj Mahal in memory of the woman he loved so much – so it has become an international symbol of love and romance.

It was built by 22,000 workers, who were helped by 1,000 elephants! It's made of the most beautiful white marble but when I arrived early in the morning, the sun was coming up and the building actually looked pink. They say that it looks even more incredibly beautiful at night when the moon is full – the whole building seems to shine. The Indians are looking after the building: cars and normal buses aren't allowed near it, to protect it from pollution. You can get there by electric bus or cycle-rickshaw. See – I know so much I could get a job as a tour guide!

I came to Agra by train. It was very busy, but not as bad as the pictures I'd seen on TV. The fast, long-distance trains are better than smaller local trains. There isn't a restaurant or café on Indian trains, but you can order food and a man brings it from the kitchen. The worst thing was no toilet paper in the toilets – you have to bring your own!

THE GOLDEN TEMPLE

Asia → India → Amritsar | 11 February

Hi everyone, and thanks for your emails. I'm glad you're enjoying my travel blog. Here I am in Amritsar in the north of India, near the Pakistan border. I've just been to see the wonderful Golden Temple. It's called Harmandir Sahib, which means 'House of God', and it's the most important place in the Sikh religion. It's an amazing place: the temple is in the middle of a lake and it really is gold! There are other buildings near the temple where you can have a vegetarian meal and even stay the night and it's all free!

SUN – HOT – BEACH – CARNIVAL

Asia → India → Goa | 17 February

Hello again – my tour continues ... I've come to the state of Goa, which is situated on the west coast of India. I'm staying in a lovely village on the coast, called Baga. Goa is famous for its fantastic beaches. It's great just to sit beside the sea and listen to the waves. You can do lots of water sport activities here too, like sailing, surfing and wind surfing. A typical meal here in Goa is fish curry and rice, which is nice – although I must say that after two weeks in India, I'm getting a bit fed up with curry ...

It's hot here – 30 °C at the moment (and February is the coldest month)! The chambermaid in my hotel told me there are three seasons in Goa: winter, summer and monsoon. The monsoon season is worse here than in Delhi: there are very heavy rains and strong winds.

I'm relaxing today but soon it won't be so quiet – the carnival starts tomorrow and will last for three days. The carnival was started by the Portuguese – Goa was one of Portugal's colonies for over 500 years. There will be lots of music, dancing and fun. I'm really looking forward to it. It'll be a great way to end my amazing holiday here in India.

Continue reading

6 a) Read Martin's travel blog. Why was Martin in India?

☐ he was visiting his family ☐ he was working there for a while

☐ he was on holiday there

b) Write the names of the three cities and one village where Martin stayed.

Martin stayed in ______________________________.

▸ S. 48

7 These sentences are wrong – write full sentences that are true.

1 Not many people speak English in Delhi.

2 The Taj Mahal was built for Mumtaz Mahal by her brother after she got married.

3 You can have a meal at the Golden Temple, but it costs a lot.

4 The monsoon season is worse in Delhi than in Goa.

8 Give information about these numbers that you find in the text. Write in German.

40

200

3 million

1000

500

• 9 Which of the four places Martin visited do you find most interesting? Why?

▸ S. 48

LISTENING

10 **What will the weather be like in Delhi? Listen to the radio report and tick the right boxes.**

Tip Listen carefully! Small words can make a big difference, e.g. *no wind* is the opposite of *a lot of wind*.

						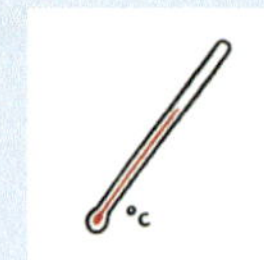
Today (Tuesday)	☐	☐	☐	☐	☐	______
Tonight	☐	☐	☐	☐	☐	______
Wednesday	☐	☐	☐	☐	☐	______
Thursday	☐	☐	☐	☐	☐	______

▸ S. 49

11 **a) Kamalika and Rajit are both 15 and live in India. Listen to them. Do they sound happy with their lives?**

Kamalika: ☐ happy / ☐ not happy

Rajit: ☐ happy / ☐ not happy

● **b) Listen again and take notes on:**

→ family • home • school • plans for the future

Kamalika

family – ______

home – ______

school – ______

future – ______

Rajit

family – ______

home – ______

school – ______

future – ______

▸ S. 49

MEDIATION

12 a) Read this article about a new type of Bollywood film.

Hollywood meets Bollywood

"Chandni Chowk to China" seems to be a typical Bollywood film: it's a musical comedy with plenty of action, songs, wonderful dances, lots of colour and beautiful women. It's made in Bollywood for the Indian market, like any other Bollywood film, but there's a big difference – the money for the film (around nine million dollars) has come from Hollywood, from the American film studio Warner Brothers. Two other Hollywood studios are also pumping money into the Indian film industry: DreamWorks has signed a $500 million deal with an Indian company, and Universal is already making Bollywood films in California.

Will these new films be box-office hits in the USA? Probably not. They come from Indian culture and are made for Indians. What's the difference? Well, says Akshay Kumar, the star of "Chandni Chowk": in a Hollywood film, if you want to say "I love you", you whisper it. In Bollywood you stand on a bridge and sing it in a loud voice! I guess that takes some getting used to! And Kumar should know – he's been in over 120 films.

So why is Hollywood interested in the Indian market? Well, it's large. Very large. India's population, about 1.13 billion people, is the second biggest population in the world. And the actors work much harder than American stars. Kumar works 12 hours a day, six days a week, so he can make six or seven films a year. No wonder the American studios are interested in Bollywood!

b) Answer the questions in German in your exercise book.

Tip
- Du darfst bei *Mediation* ein Wörterbuch zu Hilfe nehmen.
- Hier übst du das Zusammenfassen anhand von Leitfragen. Du musst dabei nicht wörtlich übersetzen.

1 Warum scheint „Chandni Chowk to China“ ein typischer Bollywood Film zu sein?
2 Wie unterscheidet er sich von anderen Bollywood Filmen?
3 Welche anderen Anzeichen gibt es, dass Hollywood sich für Bollywood interessiert?
4 Wie erklärt Akshay Kumar den Unterschied zwischen Bollywood and Hollywood Filmen?
5 Warum werden diese Filme in den USA nicht beliebt sein?
6 Wer ist Akshay Kumar?
7 Hollywood ist am indischen Markt interessiert. Gib zwei Gründe dafür. ▸ S. 50

WRITING

13 Writing letters: important words and phrases
Find the words in red and write these sentences.

1 Dear RIS or DAMMA,

2 I am writing to MOCLAINP about my stay in your TOLEH last THOMN.

3 When we arrived the room was very RITDY and the phone was SINGSIM.

4 The shower was AMAGDED too. I was very SIDPAPIONTED with the hotel.

5 Yours AFITHLLUFY,

► S. 51

● 14 You were on holiday in India last month.
Choose a letter, A or B.
Write at least 120 words.

Tip Remember:

Your address
Their address
Date
Dear ...
I am writing to ... / I want to ...

A

To:
Sunshine Holidays
139 Western Express Highway
Santacruz (East)
Mumbai 400055

- thank them for a wonderful holiday
- Lakeside Hotel very comfortable
- receptionists very friendly
- food fantastic
- beach only two minutes away
- ask them to send brochure for next year

B

To:
Buffalo Hotel
86 Juhu Tara Road
Juhu
Mumbai 400049

- complain about a meal you had there last month
- food cold
- dining room too small
- plates dirty
- toilet didn't work

► S. 51

15 **In the summer of 2008 there were especially bad floods in India. Underline the right options in the Internet news article.**

Indian TV news reported that 21 million people *have/had* suffered from winds and floods. And aid workers said that they *think/thought* that the floods *will/would* get worse.
"The government *will/would* help people who *have/had* lost their homes," the prime minister promised. He said he *will/would* visit some of the areas with floods in the next few days.

▸S. 53

16 **Write the right forms of the verbs.**

a)

Rain is filling the rivers.

Floods have damaged houses, roads and fields in 16 of India's 19 states.

The floods are destroying whole villages.

1 A news reporter said that rain ______________________ the rivers.

2 She reported that floods ______________________ houses, roads and fields in 16 of India's 19 states.

3 The news reporter said that the floods ______________________ whole villages.

b)

1 Rain ______________________ since June.

2 There ______________________ terrible floods in the next few days.

And she added that rain had fallen since June.
She reported that there would be terrible floods in the next few days.

▸S. 53

• **17** **The reporter interviewed an old man. Tell your friend what he said.**

It's terrible. I've had to leave my home and lots of people have died.

One man said that it ______________________
____
______________________.

My neighbours and I will have a lot of work to do when we go home.

He added that ______________________
____
______________________.

▸S. 53

18 **a) Which word sounds different? Cross it out.**

1 disease • trees • dress • cheese
2 down • phone • own • moan
3 mind • kind • find • wind
4 height • fight • wait • kite
5 boys • choice • noise • toys
6 store • floor • saw • power
7 crop • Dutch • govern • pump

b) Now find two words that rhyme.

1 four – *door, more*
2 loud – ____________
3 again – ____________
4 show – ____________
5 chair – ____________
6 eight – ____________
7 steel – ____________

▸ S. 55

19 **Write the opposites of these words.**

1 fortunately – ____________
2 wealthy – ____________
3 majority – ____________
4 possible – ____________
5 expensive – ____________
6 agree – ____________
7 friendly – ____________
8 entrance – ____________
9 tiny – ____________
10 dark – ____________

▸ S. 55

• **20** **Write the verbs in the *simple past* or the *past perfect* and add a reflexive pronoun (e.g. *yourself, themselves*).**

Last year my family and I had a holiday in India. We really (*enjoy*) ____________. My dad (*taught*) ____________ a little Hindi before the holiday, but most people spoke English. I took a lot of pictures with my new camera, which I (*bought*) ____________ just two days before. I got some great photos of some monkeys. We had just started a picnic when three monkeys came and (*help*) ____________ to all our food! Then my sister went for a ride on an elephant and fell off! Fortunately she (*not hurt*) ____________.

▸ S. 55

1 Kali and Chandra are British teenagers of Indian origin. Read what Kali says. Fill in the right forms of the verbs.

My friend Chandra told me that her aunt in India (*get married*) ______________ last month. She said that her new uncle (*be*) __________ a businessman and that he (*work*) ______________ in the motor industry. "They (*come*) ______________ to Britain next week," said Chandra, "so I (*meet*) ______________ him then." She added that her aunt and uncle (*arrive*) ______________ on Friday.

6 points

2 Read these definitions – what are the words?

Definitions:	Words:
1 a film that is very popular and makes a lot of money:	a ______________
2 when parents choose a husband or wife for their child:	an ______________
3 the money you earn from your job:	your ______________
4 a large shop where you can buy different sorts of things:	a ______________
5 how tall you are:	your ______________
6 you get this if you win all your races in the Olympic Games:	a ______________

6 points

3 India: a large and growing country
Write sentences about India with these words:

1 India – second biggest population – world

____

____

2 over 1500 languages – spoken – India

____

____

3 Indian businessman – own – world – biggest steel-making company

____

____

6 points

Auf den Seiten 62–63 findest du die Lösungen.

Unit 1

- **Ich kann das *past perfect* richtig verwenden:**

  Mit dem *past perfect* kann ich anzeigen, welches von mehreren Ereignissen

  ______________________________.

  Beispiel: Before I went to Dublin last May, I (*never visit*) ______________ Ireland.

- **Ich kann Bilder beschreiben:**

  – *Oben kann ich ... sehen.* ______________________________

  – *Im ersten Bild ...* ______________________________

Unit 2

- **Ich kann über die Zukunft reden:**

  Mit dem ______________ spreche ich über Ereignisse in der Zukunft, die durch einen Zeitplan festgelegt sind.

  Beispiel: ______________________________

  Mit dem ______________ sage ich, was jemand plant oder vor hat.

  Beispiel: ______________________________

Unit 3

- **Ich kann die richtigen Verbformen benutzen, um zu berichten, was jemand gesagt hat.**

  – I've bought a dog. → She told me that she ______________.

  – I'll send you a photo. → She said that she ______________.

- **Ich kann einen Brief schreiben, in dem ich mich beschwere:**

  – Anrede, wenn ich den Namen des Empfängers nicht kenne: ______________,

  – Ich möchte mich über ... beschweren: ______________

- **Ich kann stichpunktartig 15 Aussagen über Indien machen.**

  Schreibe die Aussagen in dein Heft oder auf ein Blatt Papier.

Tipp: Du kannst auch deine Lehrerin/deinen Lehrer fragen, welche Fortschritte du im Englischunterricht gemacht hast.

Unit 4

Young adults

1 Young people's problems
Circle the correct word.

1 Loren: "I love looking good, but you can't buy designer clothes *unless / because* you have lots of money – and I don't!"

2 Jake: "I'm worried because my friend is *prejudiced / addicted* to cannabis."

3 Loren: " *Inside / Instead* of complaining about teenagers, adults should try to understand us."

4 Kevin: "I get on *pretty / widely* well with my dad, but I argue with my mum."

5 Jake: "I've taken my driving test *several / selfish* times already, but I always drive badly!"

6 Kevin: "Teachers should let pupils enjoy the school holidays without homework for *once / only* ."

▸ S. 61

2 Explain the words in blue in complete sentences.

1 The media are *newspapers, magazines and television* .

2 A woman who is pregnant ______.

3 Somebody who does voluntary work ______.

4 If someone gets drunk he/she ______.

5 A teenage boy is between ______.

6 People who live in poverty ______.

7 A criminal is someone who ______.

8 You have to take a driving test before you can ______.

▸ S. 61

• 3 Why do you think some teenagers are under a lot of stress? Give reasons.

______

______

______

______

______

______

▸ S. 61

INTERPRETING

4 **a) Your British friend, Jack, is staying with you. Your friend Sara is talking to him. Her English isn't very good, so you interpret for her.**

SARA Ich laufe am nächsten Samstag in einem Rennen mit. Wünsche mir Glück!

YOU

JACK I'll cross my fingers for you. Do you do a lot of sport?

YOU

SARA Ja, ich liebe es, weil es Spaß macht, und ich fit und gesund bleibe. Was für Sachen machst du? Du kommst mir sehr fit vor.

YOU

JACK I never go running and I don't do other sports, either. I find them really boring actually – I prefer doing other things in my free time. But I go dancing twice a week and I go everywhere by bike instead of taking the bus.

YOU

b) Practise interpreting the dialogue in groups of three people. The interpreter isn't allowed to look in a workbook.

c) And you? What do you do to stay fit and healthy? ... Or what *should* you do? Make some notes and talk to a partner.

Ideas:

I ... several times a week
I probably eat too much ...
Perhaps I should ... instead of ...

▸ S. 62

PICTURE-BASED TASK – Two families

5 a) Describe what you can see in the two pictures. Read the example and look at the green box for help.

Example: *In the first picture two children are playing cards with their father. In the second picture ...*

Tip Remember to use the *present progressive* when you describe a scene, e.g. *is reading/are playing/are arguing*.

In picture A *In the first picture* *In the picture on the left*	...,	*whereas* *while*	*in picture B* *in the other one*	...
	...	*In the second picture,* *In the picture on the right,*	*on the other hand,* *in contrast,*	

b) Give your opinion.

Examples: *I think it could be somebody's birthday in picture A.*
In the second picture, the mother is perhaps saying ...
The daughter has probably ...

Tip If you don't know the English word that you want, say something else instead.
E.g.: you want to say: "The father probably thinks his daughter's *skirt* is too short." but you don't know "*skirt*" *(Rock)* → you can say: "The father probably doesn't like his daughter's clothes."

● c) Compare both scenes with your own experiences.

Example: *The first picture reminds me of last weekend, when my family ...*
When I look at the other picture, I think of when my parents ...

▸ S. 63

READING

Fashion 4 U

Teenage Style

About us | Archives | Contact us | Shop | Advertise | Subscribe

Would you buy designer knockoffs?

Is dress style important to you? Do all your friends have expensive designer clothes and gear, while you have no money and just can't afford it? What can you do? You're not going to mug anyone (we hope!), so what are your options? And just how important are designer clothes anyway?

Well, more and more, young people are turning to designer knockoffs: fake[1] designer clothes and accessories at a realistic price. Fake Gucci clothes, fake Rolex watches, fake Chanel handbags, fake Ray-Ban sunglasses ... But would you, should you wear them? Should they be banned? How do you feel when you wear them? Do they look as good as the real thing or can you tell the difference? Or are you just not bothered about designer clothes? Write in and tell us what you think.

Leave a comment

6 Responses to "Would you buy designer knockoffs?"

I have several designer things, which I love, but I also have a few designer knockoffs. I only buy fakes when I can't afford the real thing. For example, I have fake Chanel CC diamond stud earrings, but only because I can't afford the real ones! Why shouldn't I, if I like the style? However, I would never buy a fake Coach bag because the real ones aren't too expensive.

Janey – April 9 at 5.31 p.m.

In my opinion designer knockoffs should be banned. They're illegal and they steal other people's ideas. How would you like it if someone took your ideas? If you want something, you should pay for it and if you can't afford designer goods, then buy something else that looks nice and is cheaper.

Steven – April 9 at 5.37 p.m.

If people want to wear fake designer goods that's completely their choice. But I think they're naïve. They ought to realise that many fakes are made by children working in sweatshops in third world countries. By buying these designer knockoffs, you're supporting that industry. Personally I think it's wrong to buy designer knockoffs, because it's impossible to know the history of something before you buy it.

Jessica – April 9 at 5.39 p.m.

[1]fake [feɪk] *unecht; Fälschung*

I would buy knockoffs, because I don't think it's fair that it costs less than $100 to make the designer bags and then they're sold to us for $500 or something. It's ridiculous! If the retail prices were more realistic I wouldn't wear fakes because I do prefer the real thing.

Meggan – April 9 at 5.48 p.m.

I'd never buy something with a fake designer label. Why pretend that you're rich when you're not? Looking good is about taste and personal style, not how much your clothes cost and how much money you have. I can always tell which things are knockoffs anyway! Even the 'good' ones. To me it makes me think the people with the knockoffs are trying to be something they're not. It's kind of pathetic. People who wear fakes are fakes.

Samira – April 9 at 5.53 p.m.

Personally I think that when you buy a designer item, you're buying something of really good quality whereas designer knockoffs are rubbish. Buying fakes just isn't worth it, I'm afraid. They aren't well made and they fall to pieces. And you can really tell the difference: real designer goods look fantastic; the fakes just look cheap.

Simon – April 9 at 6.01 p.m.

6 a) Read the first two paragraphs. What are designer knockoffs?

- ☐ expensive clothes made by famous designers
- ☐ designer clothes that are cheap
- ☐ cheap clothes which are copies of designer clothes

b) Read the rest of the Internet forum.
What do the six people think about designer knockoffs? Tick the right opinion.

	he/she is for designer knockoffs	he/she is against designer knockoffs
Janey	☐	☐
Steven	☐	☐
Jessica	☐	☐
Meggan	☐	☐
Samira	☐	☐
Simon	☐	☐

▸S. 66

7 **Who says what? Write the right names.**

Who...

1 says that a lot of designer knockoffs are produced with child labour? ______

2 says that designer things are much too expensive? ______

3 buys real designer things if she can afford them? ______

4 says that your dress style is more important than the price of your clothes? ______

5 thinks it's stupid to buy designer knockoffs, because they aren't very good? ______

6 says that designer knockoffs aren't fair to the people who make real designer things? ______

7 thinks that you should know where something you buy has come from? ______

8 thinks that people who buy designer knockoffs want other people to think they have a lot of money? ______

8 **Read paragraphs 1 and 2 again. Explain the words below:**

1	afford *(line 3)*	If you can't afford something, you ______ .
2	mug *(line 4)*	If you mug people, ______ .
3	fake *(line 7)*	If something is fake, it ______ .
4	banned *(line 10)*	If something is banned, it ______ .

9 **Samira said "Why pretend that you're rich when you're not?" Write the sentence in German.**

______

______

______

• **10** **And you? *Do* you or *would* you buy designer knockoffs? Why?/Why not?**

______

______

______

▸ S. 66

LISTENING

11 Read the sentences first. Then listen to this radio news report and tick the right answers.

Tip Listen carefully! The speaker won't say the same words that are in this exercise.

1 The Young People's Awards took place
- [ ] a) yesterday morning.
- [ ] b) yesterday afternoon.
- [ ] c) yesterday evening.

2 The awards are for people between
- [ ] a) 5 and 17 years old.
- [ ] b) 5 and 20 years old.
- [ ] c) 5 and 21 years old.

3 Nicola started visiting the care home when
- [ ] a) her grandfather
- [ ] b) her grandmother
- [ ] c) her aunt

was there.

4 Alan Butterworth
- [ ] a) can't see.
- [ ] b) can't hear.
- [ ] c) can't swim.

5 Ali Khan phoned for
- [ ] a) the police.
- [ ] b) an ambulance.
- [ ] c) his father.

6 If you want to suggest someone for an award, send the details
- [ ] a) before 1st November.
- [ ] b) before 15th November.
- [ ] c) before 30th November.

▸ S. 67

12 A survey of five young people
a) Listen and write the two questions that they answer.

Questions:	What's ______________ ______________?	What's ______________ ______________?

b) Listen again and take notes what the young people say.

Ying	her ______________	______________
Abu	his ______________	______________
Oliver	______________	______________
Angela	______________	______________
Emily	______________	______________

c) And you? What's the best thing in your life and what's your biggest problem? Say why. Write 50 words or more.

d) Ask a partner the two questions from 12 a).

▸ S. 67

MEDIATION

13 **Your British friend, Jamie, is learning to cook healthy food at school. Read the recipe[1] he has sent you.**

Tuna & spaghetti

(serves 2 people)

1 onion
1 clove of garlic
1 red or green pepper
1 courgette
1 tin of tomatoes
1 tin of tuna
1 teaspoon of dried oregano
salt and pepper
250g dried spaghetti
Parmesan cheese

Chop the onion and fry it slowly in a little oil until it is soft, but not brown.
Chop the garlic finely and add it to the onion.
Wash and chop the pepper and courgette and add these to the onion. Fry for five minutes.
Chop the tomatoes and add them to the vegetables, then add the tuna. Put in the oregano and a little salt and pepper.
Mix everything together and cook for 15 minutes.
While the sauce is cooking, make the spaghetti:
Boil some water in a pan. Add a little salt then put in the spaghetti. Boil for 10 minutes.
Drain the spaghetti in a sieve, then serve on two plates, with the sauce over it.
Sprinkle with cheese.

a) You don't need the dictionary for some words, because they're like German or like words you already know in English.

1 oregano = *Oregano* 2 tuna = ______

3 you already know 'dry' = *trocken*, so 'dried oregano' = ______

4 'salt and pepper' = ______ und ______

b) Read the recipe. Then find words 1–4 and tick the right meaning for this text.

1 clove =	☐	*Nomen* Gewürznelke	☐	*(of garlic)* (Knoblauch-)Zehe
2 chop =	☐	*Nomen* Kotelett	☐	*Verb* klein schneiden
3 fry =	☐	*Verb* braten	☐	*Nomen* Brut
4 finely: fine =	☐	*Adjektiv* gut	☐	*Adjektiv* fein

c) Now translate the recipe into German. If you still don't understand a word, use a dictionary. ▸S. 68

[1]recipe ['resəpi] *Rezept*

WRITING – A keyword story

14 **A website for teenagers is having a writing competition. The person who writes the best story will win free driving lessons.**

a) Choose six or more of the keywords and write a story which includes them. Write at least 120 words and give your story a good title.

driving test · luck · pass · party · feel · weather · accident · lesson · optimistic · fortunately

Tips

- Decide whether you're writing about yourself or about someone else.
  *Last week **I** took **my** driving test.*
  *Last week **Jonathan** took **his** driving test.*
- Use the *simple past*, e.g. *drove, went, said.*
  But show off! Use other tenses too, e.g.
  *I **had had** over forty lessons.*
  *It **was raining** when ...*
  *I usually **drive** well, but in my test ...*
  *His mum said she **would give** him a present.*
- When you've finished, check that you've included six or more of the keywords.

b) Now read your story. Can you improve some of the sentences? Here are some ideas:

Use time phrases	*last week; half an hour later; when the test had finished; then; after that*
Write longer sentences	*I felt nervous **because** I had only had twenty lessons.* ***Although** I had only had twenty lessons, I didn't feel nervous.* *I had only had twenty lessons, **but** I didn't feel nervous.*
Use adverbs	***suddenly*** I saw ... I was ***really*** happy he ***quickly*** stopped the car he was ***incredibly*** nervous
Put in a relative clause	The man ***who*** was very friendly told him to start driving. The test ***which*** was quite hard took forty minutes.

c) Read a partner's story. Can you help him/her to improve it? ▸S. 69

15 Helen is thinking about the summer.
Complete the *if*-sentences with verbs in the *simple past*.

1 If I looked in the newspaper, I would **find** a summer job.

2 *If I found* a job, I would **work** all summer.

3 *If I* ______ all summer, I would **earn** lots of money.

4 ______ lots of money, I would **go** on holiday.

5 ______ on holiday, I would **visit** the USA.

6 ______ the USA, I would **stay** there for six weeks.

7 ______ there for six weeks, I would **have** no time for a job.

8 ______ no time for a job, I wouldn't earn any money – and I wouldn't go on holiday! Hmm ...

▸ S. 71

16 What would you do? Answer these questions.

What would you do ... / What wouldn't you do ...

→
- I would (probably / perhaps) ...
- I (probably) wouldn't ...

1 if you found € 100 in the street?

______

2 if your friend told you that he was taking drugs?

______

3 if you won € 200?

______

4 if you won € 50,000?

______

5 if you didn't have to go to school next month?

______

6 if you saw a ghost?

______

7 if you met your favourite pop star / film star?

______

8 if your brother/sister read your text messages?

______

▸ S. 71

17 Do these words rhyme? Tick the correct box.

	they rhyme	they don't rhyme
1 gone – done	☐	☐
2 afraid – made	☐	☐
3 coast – most	☐	☐
4 flood – good	☐	☐
5 peace – dress	☐	☐
6 course – horse	☐	☐
7 receive – give	☐	☐
8 fear – wear	☐	☐

▸S. 73

18 Noises in the night
Write sentences with the *past perfect* and the *simple past*.

After I *(go)* ______________ to bed last night, I *(hear)* ___________ a strange noise in the kitchen. I *(shout)* _______________ "Is anybody there?" but nobody *(answer)* _________________ . After I *(shout)* ____________________ several times, I *(get)* _________ out of bed, but the noise *(already stop)* ____ . I *(decide)* ______________ to call the police. After I *(phone)* ______________________ I *(come)* _____________ out of my bedroom. I was pretty scared, because the day before, my neighbour *(tell)* ________________ me that a burglar *(steal)* _______________ her TV and computer. Slowly I *(open)* ____________ the kitchen door. There, sitting on the kitchen table was my neighbour's cat. I *(see)* _________ that I *(leave)* _____________ the window open and the cat *(climb)* ____________________ in. I *(feel)* __________ so stupid!

▸S. 73

19 A tourist in Dublin
Put the words in the correct order and write the dialogue.

– please of tickets like the I'd bus tour for Dublin
– for each That's for adult €18 and each €7
– ticket Writer's Museum the include the Does ?
– but No, map the includes city a of it
– the long take visit does How ?
– about half The visit a and takes hours one

▸S. 73

TEST YOURSELF

1 Marcus is complaining about his family. Write the right forms of the verbs.

1 "If my dad __________ *(give)* me more pocket money, I __________ *(buy)* nicer clothes."
2 "If my brother __________ *(have)* his own bedroom, we __________ *(not argue)* so much."
3 "My sister and I __________ *(get on)* much better if she __________ *(not take)* my CDs."
4 "My parents __________ *(not be)* so grumpy all the time if they __________ *(not be)* so busy."

8 points

2 Which syllables do you stress? Say these words, then put them in the right box.

addicted • advice • argument • business • deposit • instead • motorway • pregnant
remind • result • sensible • several • sofa • teenage

O o o	o O o	O o	o O
<u>per</u>fectly	de<u>sign</u>er	<u>dri</u>ving	com<u>mit</u>
______	______	______	______
______	______	______	______
______	______	______	______
______	______	______	______

7 points

3 Write the missing verbs in these phrases.

1 ______ *a test* — *eine Prüfung machen*
2 ______ *a baby* — *ein Baby haben*
3 ______ *drunk* — *sich betrinken*
4 ______ *the point* — *nicht verstehen, worum es geht*
5 ______ *a test* — *eine Prüfung bestehen*
6 ______ *in touch* — *in Kontakt bleiben*
7 *I'll* ______ *my fingers for you* — *ich drücke dir die Daumen*
8 ______ *me luck!* — *Wünsch mir Glück!*

8 points

Auf den Seiten 63–64 findest du die Lösungen.

Unit 5

One world

1 a) Read the explanation and write the name of the problem.

1 When there isn't enough rain: *water shortage*

2 When summers get hotter and winters get colder: ____________

3 When lots of trees are cut down in the rainforest: ____________

4 When temperatures in the world rise: ____________

5 When the number of people in a country rises suddenly: ____________

6 When there isn't enough to eat: ____________

b) Look at the letters in circles and find the word:

The Atlantic, Arctic and Pacific are: ____________

▸S. 75

2 a) Find six reasons for problems and write them in your exercise book.

Tip **because** *(weil)* + **verb** phrase ... *because deserts* ***are expanding***
because of *(wegen)* + **noun** phrase ... *because of the* ***sand***

1 Millions of trees are cut down each year	because	the Gulf Stream is getting weaker.
2 Sand is now very near Beijing	because of	the country's population explosion.
3 India's carbon footprint is getting bigger		people want to use the land for farms.
4 Winters will perhaps get colder		the rising sea level.
5 Ice in the Arctic Ocean is melting		global warming.
6 The Maldives could disappear		cattle have eaten the grass next to the desert.

b) Write two more sentences about problems in the world, with *because* or *because of* in your exercise book.

▸S. 75

• 3 Why could Europe get colder? Explain this diagram which shows one reason.

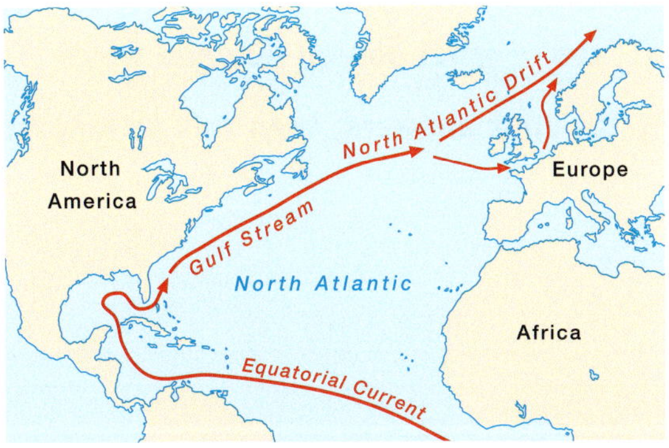

____

____

____

____

____

▸S. 75

READING

We ❤ Our Planet
washing-up liquid[2] cleans effectively, using natural ingredients – because Mother Nature knows best!

- *Friendly to the environment*
- *Kind to your hands*
- *Not tested on animals*
- *100% biodegradable*
- *No unnecessary chemicals*

Just a small amount of liquid is enough for a sink full of dishes.

We ❤ Our Planet
Washing-up liquid

with lemon & aloe vera

for people who love the planet

1 litre

We ❤ Our Planet *have been making eco-friendly products since 1985, because we believe that it's vital to look after the world we live in. We make products that are good for people, good for animals and good for the environment.*

All our packaging is made from recycled plastic, cardboard and paper.

Please recycle this bottle.

4 Read this label[1] from a bottle of washing-up liquid. Which words or phrase tell you ...

Tip
Remember:
- you can use a dictionary for reading exercises
- but you don't have to understand every word in a text in order to answer the questions.

1 when the company started?

____

2 what to do when you've used all the washing-up liquid?

____

3 that animals weren't hurt when they made this washing up liquid?

____

4 how much liquid you need when you wash up?

____

5 that it's good for your skin?

____

• **5 Do you buy things that are friendly to the environment?**

If 'yes' – what do you buy and why? **If 'no' – why not?**

Write your answers, then talk to a partner.

____

____

____

▸ S. 80

[1]label ['leɪbl] *Aufkleber; Etikett* [2]washing-up liquid ['wɒʃɪŋ ʌp 'lɪkwɪd] *Geschirrspülmittel*

A New Planet – a New Beginning?

It was a beautiful day as the astronauts stepped out of their spaceship onto the new planet. The sun was shining and the sky was bright. All around them were gigantic trees and enormous, colourful flowers. It was quiet and peaceful, like an idyllic garden.

"Be careful," said the woman. "There could be living creatures here. It looks beautiful, but don't be fooled – it could be dangerous."
"We'll take the guns," said the man.

The two explorers were on a mission. Their own planet was in trouble. The population explosion meant that there would soon not be enough land for everybody. And pollution levels had risen dramatically – if they continued to rise, the whole population would be threatened with extinction. There was only one answer: the people needed somewhere new to live: a new world for a new beginning. And reports had suggested that this planet could be perfect ...

The explorers walked for three days, camping overnight. The days were short on this planet; much shorter than at home, but the astronauts were still tired. They were hot in their protective space suits and large helmets, and the food and drink and canisters of air which they carried on their backs were heavy. They were nervous too. What if they met some sort of wild animal? It could attack them, even kill them. But they couldn't allow themselves to be afraid. They *had* to do this for the people back home. Still, they were optimistic. Plants grew here, like at home, so there must be rain here too.

But on the fourth day, things changed.

"Look! Over here!" shouted the man. There, on the ground in front of him, lay a strange, white skeleton. What kind of animal had it been?
"Here's another!" shouted the woman. "And three more ..." She stopped suddenly. "What's *that*?!"
There was something large in the distance. As they walked towards it, they saw that it was an enormous, square, black building.
"So there *is* intelligent life here!" said the man. "Or at least there *was* ..."
"What could this building be?" wondered the woman. She turned on the machine she was carrying.
Click click click click ...
As they walked closer to the building, the clicking noise grew louder and louder.
"There's a lot of radioactivity here. Too much – it's dangerous. Let's get back."

On the way back they found a river. The woman held the machine close to the water. *Click click click* ... Radioactive. Back at the spaceship she held the machine close to the ground. *Click click click* ... "The planet is contaminated with radioactivity," said the man sadly. "It's unsafe, totally uninhabitable."
How were they going to tell the people back home that their hopes for a new beginning here were now completely destroyed? They would have to start again, travel even further, try to find somewhere else.

Sadly, the man and woman left planet Earth and began the long journey back to their home planet, one of the 63 moons of Jupiter.

6 **Read the short story and answer the questions. Tick the right answer.**

Tip You can use a dictionary.

1 What kind of story is it?
- [ ] a) romantic
- [ ] b) science-fiction
- [ ] c) funny

2 When does the story take place?
- [ ] a) in the past
- [ ] b) in the present
- [ ] c) in the future

7 **True, false or not in the text? Tick the right answer.**

	True	False	Not in text
1 It was sunny when the astronauts arrived on the planet.	☐	☐	☐
2 They took guns with them because they had seen animals.	☐	☐	☐
3 The man and woman were married.	☐	☐	☐
4 They were exploring because there would soon be too many people on their home planet.	☐	☐	☐
5 The days on their home planet were longer.	☐	☐	☐
6 The water in the river was safe to drink.	☐	☐	☐
7 The man and woman stayed on the planet for three days.	☐	☐	☐
8 Their home planet was planet Earth.	☐	☐	☐

8 **Answer the following questions in English. You don't have to write full sentences. Then write the line where you found the information.**

1 How many astronauts were there? ____________________

2 What were the astronauts wearing? ____________________

3 What did the man find on the fourth day? ____________________

4 Why was the planet uninhabitable? ____________________

____

• **9** **Write the last sentence of the story in German.**

____

____

____

▸S. 80

LISTENING

10 You're visiting a British school. Listen to two announcements made by the head teacher. Write the information.

1st Announcement

Talk about: ____________________

Where: ____________________

When: ____________________

2nd Announcement

Meeting of: ____________________

When: ____________________

Where: ____________________

Do what: ____________________

▸ S. 81

11 a) Listen to the discussion. Tick the right answer.

1 Where's the discussion taking place? ☐ a) in a school ☐ b) on a bus ☐ c) on the radio

2 Does Sandra like the first book? ☐ a) yes ☐ b) no

3 Does Mike like the second book? ☐ a) yes ☐ b) no

4 What are the two books about? ☐ a) what to eat ☐ b) how to live ☐ c) world problems

b) These sentences are wrong. Cross out the mistakes and correct them.

Tip Read the sentences before you listen:
- they help you to understand the discussion,
- they show you what details to listen for.

1 The first book, Change the World for a Fiver, was written by one person.

2 It's a British book and it costs nine pounds.

3 The book is about helping other people, helping animals and helping yourself.

4 Two of the ideas are: learn to be friendly in another language and make someone dance.

5 The second book, Screw It, Let's Do It, was written by a famous sportsman.

6 He'd recommend it for everybody, but especially for teachers.

▸ S. 81

MEDIATION

12 a) Look at the poster and the job advert.

WE'VE GOT PROBLEMS!

- Every year millions of people suffer from water shortages in Africa and the Middle East.
- Climate change threatens the work of farmers in the Third World.
- And wealthy countries' carbon footprints are getting larger and larger.

BE PART OF THE SOLUTION!

Together we can change the world. Are we totally unrealistic?
No, the **One Planet 4 Us** organisation has already raised millions of pounds
– for water aid in Third World countries
– for 'green' education programmes here in the UK.

HOW CAN YOU HELP?

You can help by sending money or doing voluntary work, for example.
For more information go to our website: **www.OnePlanet4Us.org.uk**

One Planet 4 Us* – *summer job

We are looking for a young person to come and help in our office for three days a week during the summer holidays. The job involves answering the phone and general office work. You must know how to use a computer. You must be over 16 and have a pleasant, friendly personality.

For more information and an application form please phone Sue Smith on 0845 455 293, Mondays to Thursdays, 10 a.m. – 4 p.m.

One Planet 4 Us, 23 Green Ave, London, W6 9LM

b) Answer these questions in German.

Tip You can use a dictionary, but try answering the questions without one first.

1 Welche drei Probleme werden im Poster erwähnt?
2 Was hat die Organisation *One Planet 4 Us* schon erreicht?
3 Wie können Menschen mithelfen?
4 Welche Informationen über den Job sind in der Anzeige enthalten?
5 Was wird von den Bewerbern verlangt?
6 Wann kann man Sue Smith anrufen?

► S. 82

WRITING – Formal letters

13 Important words and phrases
Write these sentences or phrases in the right order.

1 Sir Madam, or Dear

____

2 newspaper I advert in saw the your

____

3 would the like job apply for to I

____

5 an holidays I in office worked the Christmas during

____

6 English happy my teacher referee be would be My to

____

7 pay know Please much let how me you

____

8 I'm you hearing forward to from looking

____

14 a) Look again at the *One Planet 4 Us* job advert on page 54.
Write a letter to apply for the job.
Add some information about yourself:

- What's your age?
- Where do you live?
- Do you have any work experience?
- Why are you interested in the job?

Tip After you've written your letter, check the spelling and grammar.

b) Now check a partner's letter.

- Has he/she given enough information?
- Are the spelling and grammar correct?

▸ S. 83

15 **"A Visit to the Future"**
There's a short story competition in a magazine.
Look at the picture and write a story of at least 120 words.

Tip Remember, don't describe the picture – make up a story. It must have a beginning, a middle and an end.

Ideas:
- Who went on a 'visit to the future'? Give details.
- Did he/she go alone or with anybody else?
- How did he/she/they get there?
- What did he/she see?
- What was different in the future?
- What were people doing?
- What things happened while he/she was there?
- Did anything exciting happen?
- Did he/she meet anybody interesting?
- Say what people said and thought, e.g.: *"I'm scared," said her friend. "I want to go home."* or *Her friend said that she felt scared and she wanted to go home.*
- How did he/she/they feel ... during the visit?
  ... after the visit?

Tip
- Use time phrases, e.g.:
  after that; later; then; suddenly; that evening; the next day
- Write longer sentences. Join sentences with words like
  although; because; but; which
- Make your story better: use adjectives and adverbs, e.g.
  clean; strange; funny; happy; busy; friendly; quiet
  fortunately; suddenly; quickly; slowly; quietly; loudly

▸S. 83

16 Change the verbs: Use the right passive forms.

1 Many people consider deforestation as one of the biggest problems today.
→ Deforestation ______________ by many people as one of the biggest problems today.
2 Every day we lose 137 different sorts of plants and animals from the rainforest – for ever.
→ Every day 137 different sorts of plants and animals ______________ from the rainforest – for ever.
3 They have cut down 130,000 square kilometres of forest in the last 10 years.
→ 130,000 square kilometres of forest ______________ in the last 10 years.
4 World leaders will discuss deforestation at a meeting next month.
→ Deforestation ______________ by world leaders at a meeting next month.

▸S. 85

17 a) Write the verbs, using the passive forms in the right tenses.

The Maldives is a country of over 1000 small islands in the Indian Ocean. Last year it ______________ (*visit*) by more than 600,000 tourists. Now, however, it ______________ (*threaten*) by rising sea levels. The sea has already risen 15 cm – this ______________ (*cause*) by global warming over a number of years. If the sea rises more the Maldives ______________ (*cover*) by water and its people ______________ (*leave*) without homes.

• b) Write these sentences in the passive. You don't always need to form them with 'by'.

1 The government see this as serious risk. → *This is* ______________
______________.
2 They have saved money. → ______________.
3 If necessary, they'll buy land in another country. → *If necessary,* ______________
______________.
4 Of course they hope that they won't need these plans. → *Of course they hope that* ______________
______________.
5 The country has already had problems. In 2004 a terrible tsunami damaged the tourist industry. → *In 2004* ______________.

▸S. 87

18 **What are the sounds of the words marked in red? Tick the right sound.**

a)

	[g]	or	[dʒ]
1 intelligent	☐		☐
2 disadvantage	☐		☐
3 guided	☐		☐
4 religion	☐		☐
5 gym	☐		☐
6 ghost	☐		☐

b)

	[aɪ]	or	[ɪ]
7 fight	☐		☐
8 quick	☐		☐
9 mind	☐		☐
10 primary	☐		☐
11 fifty	☐		☐
12 middle	☐		☐

▸ S. 87

19 **Write words that mean the same.**

1 rich – ____________
2 terrible – ____________
3 get bigger – ____________
4 somebody – ____________
5 also – ____________
6 go up – ____________
7 completely – ____________
8 big – ____________

▸ S. 87

20 **a) Some people in Pripyat were asked: "What were you doing when you heard the explosion at Chernobyl nuclear power station?" Write their answers.**

→ was/were + verb + *ing*

1

I ____________
____________.

2

I ____________
____________.

3

We ____________
____________.

b) An old man was interviewed. What did he say? Use reported speech.

It isn't easy – I feel very sad because I've lost my home. I hope an accident like this will never happen again.

He said that ____________
____
____
____

▸ S. 87

1 Look at the pictures. Write the names of the problems.

1
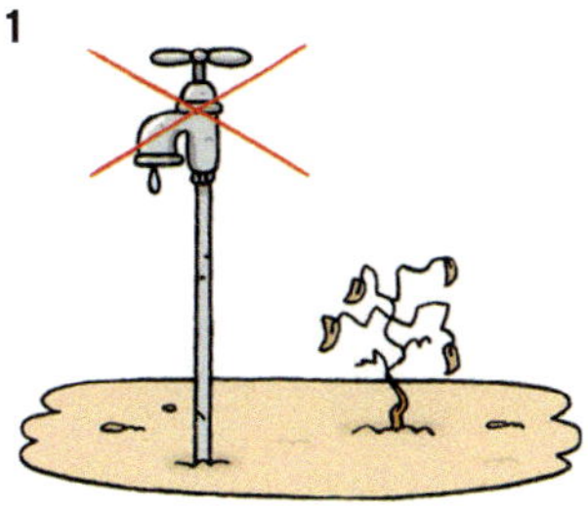

2

3

4

5
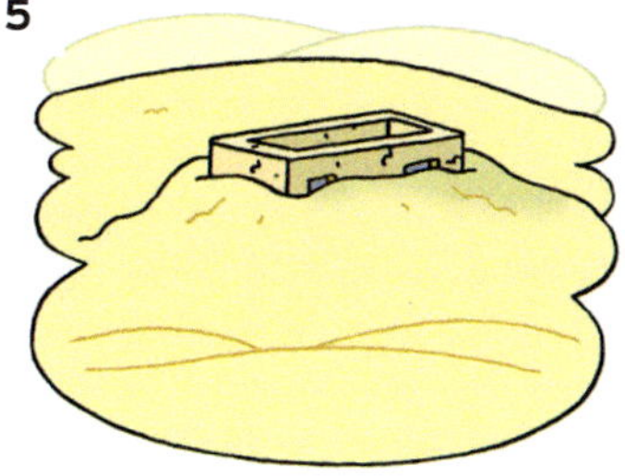

6

6 points

2 Write the verbs, using the right passive forms (*present, past, future*).

Pripyat, in Ukraine, is a ghost town. In April 1986 the town ______ (*contaminate*) by radioactive gases from an explosion at the Chernobyl nuclear power station. People ______ (*evacuate*) from the town, but since 1986 hundreds of people ______ (*kill*) by diseases like cancer and leukaemia which ______ (*cause*) by the radioactivity. Nobody lives in Pripyat today. Nobody knows how long it ______ (*contaminate*) and when it will be safe to return. However, the town has become a strange tourist attraction: it ______ (*visit*) by about a hundred tourists every year.

6 points

3 What are these people saying about the environment? Find the right sentences.

1 "What I find	☐ worth doing	☐ to reduce your	☐ abroad."
2 "You simply can't	☐ that what each person	☐ how much carbon dioxide	☐ can."
3 "That's no excuse	☐ would rather	☐ producing	☐ so little effect."
4 "Many people	☐ frightening is	☐ what you	☐ carbon footprint."
5 "The trouble is	☐ live without	☐ can do has	☐ we produce."
6 "It's still	☐ for not trying	☐ have a holiday	☐ carbon dioxide."

Auf Seite 64 findest du die Lösungen.

9 points

Unit 4

Ich kann Sätze mit *if* bilden.

Mit *if*-Sätzen vom Typ II kann ich sagen, was unter bestimmten Bedingungen passieren würde.

if + simple ______ + would

Beispiel: ____

____

Ich kann einen formellen Brief schreiben.

– Ich möchte mich auf die Stelle bewerben. ____________________

____

– Ich freue mich auf eine Nachricht von Ihnen. ____________________

____

– Ich möchte ein Doppelzimmer buchen. ____________________

____

– Lassen Sie mich wissen ... ____________________

Unit 5

Ich weiß, warum man das Passiv verwendet.

Mit dem Passiv sage ich, dass etwas mit ____________ oder ____________ gemacht wird oder ____________. Das Wort ______ zeigt an, von wem die Handlung ausgeführt wird.

Ich kann das Passiv mit Verben in der Gegenwart, in der Vergangenheit und in der Zukunft verwenden.

Beispiele:

trees absorb carbon dioxide → carbon dioxide ____________ by trees

Turkey built dams on its rivers → dams ____________ on Turkey's rivers

we have reduced our carbon footprint → our carbon footprint ____________

we will make more progress → more progress ____________

Tipp: Du kannst auch deine Lehrerin/deinen Lehrer fragen, welche Fortschritte du im Englischunterricht gemacht hast.

Wenn du Probleme bei der Punktevergabe hast, bitte deine Lehrerin / deinen Lehrer um Hilfe.*

Unit 1 – Seite 12

1 My family

1 I'm American but my *ancestors* are Irish.
2 They *emigrated* to the USA in 1854.
3 In Ireland they had to *rent* their land
4 from a *landowner*, but in the USA
5 they were able to *own* some land.
6 They *planted* vegetables and they soon had a successful business.

Gib dir für jede richtige Lösung 1 Punkt.
Deine Punktzahl:

2 Which syllables do you stress?

O o o	o O o
company	important
industry	*injustice*
Netherlands	*republic*
president	
Protestant	
o O o o	**o o O o**
receptionist	independent
celebrity	*European*
enormously	*idealistic*
minority	*population*

Gib dir für jedes richtige Wort 0,5 Punkte.
Deine Punktzahl:

3 My grandparents

1 My grandparents *came* to California from New York in 1963.
2 They *had met* six years before and *had married* in 1959,
3 while they *were living* in New York.
4 They *had* their first child, my father, in California.
5 My grandfather *was working* as taxi-driver when my father was born.

Gib dir für jede richtige Lösung 1 Punkt.
Deine Punktzahl:

Zähle alle Punkte zusammen.
Von insgesamt 18 Punkten hast du erreicht:

TESTERGEBNIS

18–16 Punkte:
Du bist richtig fit in Englisch. Mache weiter so!

15,5–13,5 Punkte:
Deine Englischkenntnisse sind gut. Versuche die kleinen Fehler noch zu vermeiden.

13–10 Punkte:
Du kannst schon recht gut Englisch. Aber du musst noch genauer lernen, um besser zu werden.

9,5–6,5 Punkte:
Du kannst einiges in Englisch. Leider hast du noch einige Lücken. Frage deine Lehrerin / deinen Lehrer, wie du diese Lücken schließen kannst.

6–0 Punkte:
Leider hat es dieses Mal nicht so gut geklappt. Du hast noch erhebliche Lücken. Frage deine Lehrerin / deinen Lehrer, wie du diese Lücken schließen kannst.

Unit 2 – Seite 24

1 Read the phonetic script and write the names of these animals in English.

1 *monkey*
2 *buffalo*
3 *elephant*
4 *leopard*
5 *lion*
6 *rhinoceros*

Gib dir für jedes richtige Wort 0,5 Punkte.
Deine Punktzahl:

* Bei der Bewertung der Übungen mit Punkten wurde in der Regel nach folgenden Kriterien vorgegangen: Für ein Lösungswort, das nur zugeordnet werden muss, gibt es 0,5 Punkte. Bei einem selbstständig zu schreibenden Lösungswort oder einem Satz, der nur zugeordnet werden muss, 1 Punkt, bei der selbstständigen Formulierung eines ganzen Satzes 2 Punkte.

2 South Africa today

South Africa is often called the rainbow *nation* because of all the different cultures of the people *who/that* live there. The *Whites* speak English or Afrikaans which is a language like *Dutch*. The Blacks speak more than nine *different* languages. But South Africa still *has* problems. Unemployment has been *going* down but 23% of people still have no *job*. Only 74.4% of houses have *running* water and 20% of houses don't have *electric* light.

Gib dir für jede richtige Lösung 1 Punkt.
Deine Punktzahl:

3 Jacob asks Amy what she's doing at the weekend.

1 *On Saturday morning I'm playing the guitar.*
2 *In the afternoon I'm visiting my aunt and uncle.*
3 *On Saturday evening I'm babysitting.*
4 *On Sunday morning I'm going fishing with my/a friend).*

Gib dir für jeden richtigen Satz 2 Punkte.
Deine Punktzahl:

4 a) Read the article.

1 *True* 2 *False* 3 *False* 4 *False*
5 *Not in text* 6 *False* 7 *Not in text*
8 *True*

Gib dir für jede richtige Lösung 1 Punkt.
Deine Punktzahl:

b) Numbers

1st = *first* 2nd = *second* 3rd = *third*
4th = *fourth* *6th* = sixth

Gib dir für jedes richtige Wort 0,5 Punkte.
Deine Punktzahl:

Zähle alle Punkte zusammen.
Von insgesamt 31,5 Punkten hast du erreicht:

TESTERGEBNIS

31,5–28 Punkte:
Du bist richtig fit in Englisch. Mache weiter so!

27,5–23,5 Punkte:
Deine Englischkenntnisse sind gut. Versuche die kleinen Fehler noch zu vermeiden.

23–17,5 Punkte:
Du kannst schon recht gut Englisch. Aber du musst noch genauer lernen, um besser zu werden.

17–11,5 Punkte:
Du kannst einiges in Englisch. Leider hast du noch einige Lücken. Frage deine Lehrerin / deinen Lehrer, wie du diese Lücken schließen kannst.

11–0 Punkte:
Leider hat es dieses Mal nicht so gut geklappt. Du hast noch erhebliche Lücken. Frage deine Lehrerin / deinen Lehrer, wie du diese Lücken schließen kannst.

Unit 3 – Seite 35

1 Kali and Chandra are British teenagers of Indian origin.

My friend Chandra told me that her aunt in India *had got married* last month. She said that her new uncle *was* a businessman and that he *worked* in the motor industry.
"They*'re/are coming* to Britain next week," said Chandra, "so I*'ll / 'm going to meet* him then." She added that her aunt and uncle *would arrive / were arriving* on Friday.

Gib dir für jede richtige Lösung 1 Punkt.
Deine Punktzahl:

2 **Read these definitions – what are the words?**

1 a *box-office hit*
2 an *arranged marriage*
3 your *salary*
4 a *department store*
5 your *height*
6 a *gold medal*

Gib dir für jede richtige Lösung 1 Punkt.
Deine Punktzahl:

3 **India: a large and growing country**

1 *India has the second biggest population in the world.*
2 *Over 1500 languages are spoken in India.*
3 *An Indian businessman owns the world's biggest steel-making company.*

Gib dir für jeden richtigen Satz 2 Punkte.
Deine Punktzahl:

Zähle alle Punkte zusammen. Von insgesamt 18 Punkten hast du erreicht:

TESTERGEBNIS

18–16 Punkte:
Du bist richtig fit in Englisch. Mache weiter so!

15–13 Punkte:
Deine Englischkenntnisse sind gut. Versuche die kleinen Fehler noch zu vermeiden.

12–10 Punkte:
Du kannst schon recht gut Englisch. Aber du musst noch genauer lernen, um besser zu werden.

9–7 Punkte:
Du kannst einiges in Englisch. Leider hast du noch einige Lücken. Frage deine Lehrerin / deinen Lehrer, wie du diese Lücken schließen kannst.

6–0 Punkte:
Leider hat es dieses Mal nicht so gut geklappt. Du hast noch erhebliche Lücken. Frage deine Lehrerin / deinen Lehrer, wie du diese Lücken schließen kannst.

Unit 4 – Seite 48

1 **Marcus is complaining about his family.**

1 "If my dad *gave* me more pocket money, I *would/could buy* nicer clothes."
2 "If my brother *had* his own bedroom, we *wouldn't argue* so much."
3 "My sister and I *would get on* much better if she *didn't take* my CDs."
4 "My parents *wouldn't be* so grumpy all the time if they *weren't* so busy."

Gib dir für jede richtige Lösung 1 Punkt.
Deine Punktzahl:

2 **Which syllables do you stress?**

O o o	o O o
perfectly	designer
argument	*addicted*
motorway	*deposit*
sensible	
several	

O o	o O
driving	commit
business	*advice*
pregnant	*instead*
teenage	*remind*
sofa	*result*

Gib dir für jedes richtige Wort 0,5 Punkte.
Deine Punktzahl:

3 **Write the missing verbs in these phrases.**

1 *take* a test
2 *have* a baby
3 *get* drunk
4 *miss* the point
5 *pass* a test
6 *keep* in touch
7 I'll *cross* my fingers for you
8 *Wish* me luck!

Gib dir für jede richtige Lösung 1 Punkt.
Deine Punktzahl:

Zähle alle Punkte zusammen.
Von insgesamt 23 Punkten
hast du erreicht:

TESTERGEBNIS

23–21 Punkte:
Du bist richtig fit in Englisch. Mache weiter so!

20,5–17 Punkte:
Deine Englischkenntnisse sind gut. Versuche die kleinen Fehler noch zu vermeiden.

16,5–12 Punkte:
Du kannst schon recht gut Englisch. Aber du musst noch genauer lernen, um besser zu werden.

11,5–8 Punkte:
Du kannst einiges in Englisch. Leider hast du noch einige Lücken. Frage deine Lehrerin / deinen Lehrer, wie du diese Lücken schließen kannst.

7,5–0 Punkte:
Leider hat es dieses Mal nicht so gut geklappt. Du hast noch erhebliche Lücken. Frage deine Lehrerin / deinen Lehrer, wie du diese Lücken schließen kannst.

Unit 5 - Seite 59

1 Look at the pictures. Write the names of the problems.

1 *water shortage*
2 *deforestation*
3 *global warming / climate change*
4 *population explosion*
5 *expanding deserts*
6 *rising sea level(s)*

Gib dir für jede richtige Lösung 1 Punkt. Deine Punktzahl:

2 Write the verbs, using the right passive forms (*present, past, future*).
Pripyat, in Ukraine, is a ghost town. In April 1986 the town *was contaminated* by radioactive gases from an explosion at the Chernobyl nuclear power station. People *were evacuated* from the town, but since 1986 hundreds of people *have been killed* by diseases like cancer and leukaemia which *were / have been caused* by the radioactivity. Nobody lives in Pripyat today. Nobody knows how long it *will be contaminated* and when it will be safe to return. However, the town has become a strange tourist attraction: it *is visited* by about a hundred tourists every year.

Gib dir für jede richtige Lösung 1 Punkt. Deine Punktzahl:

3 What are these people saying about the environment? Find the right sentences.

1 *"What I find frightening is how much carbon dioxide we produce."*
2 *"You simply can't live without producing carbon dioxide."*
3 *"That's no excuse for not trying to reduce your carbon footprint."*
4 *"Many people would rather have a holiday abroad."*
5 *"The trouble is that what each person can do has so little effect."*
6 *"It's still worth doing what you can."*

Gib dir für jeden richtigen Satz 1,5 Punkte. Deine Punktzahl:

Zähle alle Punkte zusammen.
Von insgesamt 21 Punkten
hast du erreicht:

TESTERGEBNIS

21–19 Punkte:
Du bist richtig fit in Englisch. Mache weiter so!

18,5–16 Punkte:
Deine Englischkenntnisse sind gut. Versuche die kleinen Fehler noch zu vermeiden.

15,5–11 Punkte:
Du kannst schon recht gut Englisch. Aber du musst noch genauer lernen, um besser zu werden.

10,5–7 Punkte:
Du kannst einiges in Englisch. Leider hast du noch einige Lücken. Frage deine Lehrerin / deinen Lehrer, wie du diese Lücken schließen kannst.

6,5–0 Punkte:
Leider hat es dieses Mal nicht so gut geklappt. Du hast noch erhebliche Lücken. Frage deine Lehrerin / deinen Lehrer, wie du diese Lücken schließen kannst.